This book belongs to...

Name:..

Age:..

Published by Dennis Publishing Ltd. 30 Cleveland St, London W1T 4JD. Company registered in England. www.dennis.co.uk

DISCLAIMER
The screenshots shown in this publication were taken from Minecraft, a game published by Mojang Synergies AB. Game design, programming and graphics for Minecraft were authored by Notch, employees and/or freelancers of Mojang Synergies AB. "Minecraft" is a registered trademark of Mojang Synergies AB. This publication and its contents are not licensed, authorised or connected with Mojang Synergies or any other individuals who are authors of Minecraft. This is a 100% unofficial and independent publication.
   Dennis Publishing excludes all liability for the content and service provided by and websites we review. We are not responsible for and do not endorse any advertising, products or resources available from such external resources or websites and shall not be liable to any party as a result of any information, services or resources made available through such websites.

All copyrights recognised and used specifically for the purpose of criticism and review.

MINECRAFT SECRETS & CHEATS 2018

WHAT'S INSIDE?!

101 BRILLIANT MINECRAFT TRICKS!
Give yourself a head start at Minecraft!
Pages 10, 22, 34

THE ADVENTURES OF CRAFTY CALLUM!
See what trouble he gets into on page 38!

THE CRAZIEST BUILDS!
Reckon you can beat any of these?!
Page 18

AMAZING TIPS!
Get the best potions on page 32, epic recipes on page 42 and brilliant enchantments on page 44!

PUZZLES You'll find loads of puzzles dotted around this annual – and all the answers are on page 60!

THE 10 MUST-KNOW CHARACTERS OF MINECRAFT

Steve

Alex

Creeper

STEVE

First introduced to Minecraft in the very first PC version way back in December 2010, Steve was the only default skin for the player for almost four years. Steve has blue eyes and short brown hair, and wears a light blue T-shirt, blue jeans and grey shoes. The original version of Steve had a dark brown goatee beard, and this version of the skin has the nickname "Char" after the original template's filename.

ALEX

Alex was added to Minecraft in PC version 1.8 pre1, which was released in August 2014, and then quickly added to the Console and Pocket editions. Alex has green eyes and long ginger hair, which she wears in a ponytail. She wears a green tunic with a belt around the waist, brown leggings and grey boots. Her character model has thinner arms than Steve, but this is the only difference between the two.

CREEPER

The creeper is Minecraft's signature villain! These weird monsters hide in the dark, and when they see an enemy – meaning you – they hiss loudly before exploding! They don't have any mercy and can't be reasoned with, and they're scared of only one thing: cats. All you can do is avoid them or run. Minecraft's creators say that if you touched a creeper it would feel like wet leaves, but why would you get that close?!

Witch

Zombie villager

Iron golem

WITCH

The witch was an ordinary villager until she got struck by lightning! Turned evil by the strike, she was banished from the village to live in a swamp. She had to build her hut on stilts to keep the water out, and she spends her time brewing potions in her cauldron so that she can get revenge on the villagers who cast her out!

ZOMBIE VILLAGER

When a zombie plague attacked their village, these unfortunate souls were caught and bitten. It didn't take them long to join the zombie ranks, but hope isn't lost – somewhere inside each of these zombie villagers lies the person they once were. With a little magic, some kind players are able to cure the zombie disease and bring them back to the realm of the living.

IRON GOLEM

Built by friendly villagers, the iron golem was brought to life using magic, and now protects large villages against attacks from zombies and witches, or anything else that would injure its masters.

ZOMBIE PIGMAN

The zombie pigman lives in the Nether. Half-zombie, half-pig, all it remembers is enjoying its life in the Overworld, eating potatoes and carrots, before a bright flash of light changed everything for it. Now the pigman lives in the Nether, trying to find a portal to return to the Overworld and attacking anything that gets in his way with his golden sword.

Zombie pigman

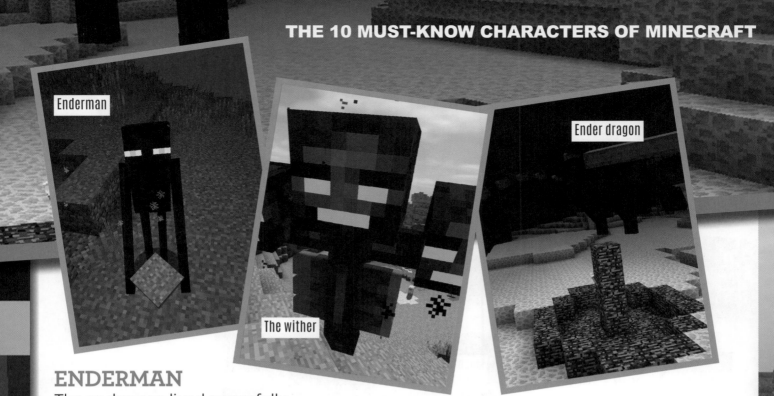

Enderman

The wither

Ender dragon

ENDERMAN

The endermen lived peacefully with one another in the End, their realm protected by the ender dragon, but one day invaders visited their world and began to take their precious artifacts, such as the elytra. Now they're fighting back, using their teleportation powers to visit the Overworld and even travelling as far as the Nether to eliminate anyone who might try to attack them.

THE WITHER

Formed from the heads of three wither skeletons and the strange soul sand that exists only in the Nether, the wither is a vengeful and dangerous creature with the ability to summon a destructive wither storm that decimates everything in its path. The keeper of the rare and powerful Nether star, it's almost impossible to defeat – just being near it makes you feel weak!

The knowledge of how to summon the wither was considered so dangerous that centuries ago the ancient inhabitants of the Overworld tried to hide it completely, but one painting gives clues as to how you might bring the wither to life. Only the very brave or incredibly stupid would try...

ENDER DRAGON

The guardian of the End, no-one knows whether the ender dragon is enslaved by the endermen, or if it was placed there to keep them from escaping their realm. Either way, its powerful attacks can only be defeated by the strongest of warriors, and its dragon's breath can power up any potion in ways few sorcerers get to try. Although the dragon can be killed, it always leaves behind an egg that can be hatched by those who know how to use the mysterious End crystals.

Be warned, though: don't ever fight the dragon if you don't expect to win, because once you're in the End there's no way out without someone dying, whether that's you or the dragon itself!

101 MINECRAFT TRICKS PART 1

Do you think you know every trick, shortcut and secret technique in Minecraft? We bet you don't, so we're going to share our expert wisdom with you. Here are 101 tricks the experts have been keeping all to themselves!

1 If you want to grow mushrooms, you can plant them on podzol and mycelium, and they'll stay where they are even in direct sunlight. Mycelium spreads to nearby dirt blocks, but podzol doesn't.

2 You might think cobblestone is useless, but it's actually one of the most useful blocks in the game and features in at least 17 recipes! So don't throw it away too quickly.

3 You can create your own grass paths by right-clicking with the shovel on grass-covered blocks (or pressing the assigned "use" button) instead of digging with it.

Mushrooms on podzol and mycelium

You can make your own paths

You can't drown in lava!

4 If you're not standing on something while underwater (i.e. sinking or swimming), blocks take 25 times as long to break, so don't waste your time trying to mine or dig while swimming!

5 Even though it's a liquid, it's not possible to drown in lava, though obviously you need some heavy protection to stay alive in it...!

6 Packed ice blocks don't melt even if placed next to a light source. Unfortunately, the only way to get them (except in Creative mode) is to mine them using a Silk Touch pickaxe from an ice spike, so they're very rare!

7 If you collect a raw ore block (for example, if you use a Silk Touch pickaxe) you don't have to place it then mine it again – you can smelt it into its resource.

Burn wood effectively

Jungle trees drop fewer saplings than most

Snow layers are uneven

8 Wood blocks can be used as fuel in furnaces, but it's more efficient to craft them into planks then burn them.

9 Wood planks are the single most useful block in the game, featuring in 28 different recipes.

10 Destroying a leaf block drops a sapling one in every 20 times. Jungle leaves only drop a sapling one in every 40 times.

11 Redstone ore will give off low-level light (level 9) for around a minute if struck or walked over by the player or a mob. If there's redstone nearby in a dark area, you can hit it while mining to save using up a valuable torch.

12 Snow layers can be stacked up to create partial blocks. Eight layers create a full-size snow block.

You can dry out wet sponges

Stairs save you energy

13 Even though cacti damage players and mobs that come into contact with them, you can mine cacti with your hand without taking any injuries.

14 Grass only spreads to dirt if there's a light level of at least 4 on both blocks, but mycelium only spreads to dirt if the light level is at least 9 on both blocks.

15 You can cook a wet sponge in a furnace, which will dry it out again!

16 If there's an empty bucket in the fuel slot when a furnace finishes drying out a sponge, it will turn it into a bucket of water.

17 Stairs aren't just useful for decoration or because they're compact – they also reduce your hunger stat less than jumping the same distance up or down would.

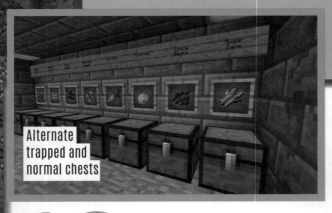
Alternate trapped and normal chests

18 Two chests placed next to each other will form a double chest, and then you have to leave a gap between a double chest and a normal chest. However, you can place a trapped chest next to a normal chest, which is a good way to maximise storage space.

19 Four iron bars in a square will create a gap big enough for the player and other mobs to drop through, but it will repel water and lava because the gap is offset from the normal block grid.

20 You can craft glowstone blocks without ever leaving the Overworld by killing witches and collecting the glowstone dust that they drop.

21 You can put carpet or snow on top of soul sand to negate its effects.

22 You can't craft cracked stone bricks, but you can turn stone bricks into cracked stone bricks by smelting them in a furnace.

23 If you fall onto a slime block, you'll bounce and won't take any damage.

24 Jack o' lanterns can be used to create snow and iron golems the same way pumpkins can.

25 Carpets let light through, so you can place carpet on top of glowstone to make a room appear illuminated even if there's no obvious light source.

26 Resource blocks like iron, gold, emerald, coal and diamond contain nine pieces of their respective resource (i.e. there are nine gold ingots in a block of gold). However, they stack in piles of 64, so you can effectively carry 576 ingots/gems in one inventory slot.

Witches drop glowstone

Carpets let light through

Slime blocks make you bounce!

Mushrooms also grow in flower pots

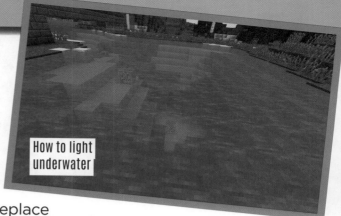

How to light underwater

27 Rather than putting coal in your furnaces, craft a block of coal and use that instead. It burns for as long as 10 pieces of coal would, so since it only takes nine pieces to make you technically get a bonus piece!

28 If there's a hole within six blocks of a water source block, the flow is directed towards it.

29 When you're decorating your base, remember that you can put more than just flowers in flower pots. They can also hold mushrooms, grass and ferns, saplings (which never grow) and even cacti!

30 Consider building your base in the side of a mountain. There'll be fewer ways for mobs to sneak up on you, and you'll get easy access to minerals like coal and iron ore without having to travel deep underground.

31 If you want a fire that never goes out, set Netherrack on fire. You can use this technique to create an incinerator, build a working fireplace or just use it as some dramatic decoration.

32 If you want to light underwater, use glowstone blocks or (if you haven't reached the Nether yet) Jack o' lanterns. Both of these blocks emit light even stronger than a torch and don't get extinguished underwater.

33 You can make copies of books and maps (either for backups or sharing with other players) by crafting them with a blank version of what they are.

34 You can place a clock inside an item frame to create a wall clock, which lets you see how long you've got until it gets dark (or light!) without taking up valuable space in your inventory.

MORE ON P22

Netherrack burns forever

You can put clocks in frames

ME IN

Grab your pens and pencils: these two pictures need your help! Can you colour them in and make them awesome?

PUZZLE

Dot-To-Dot

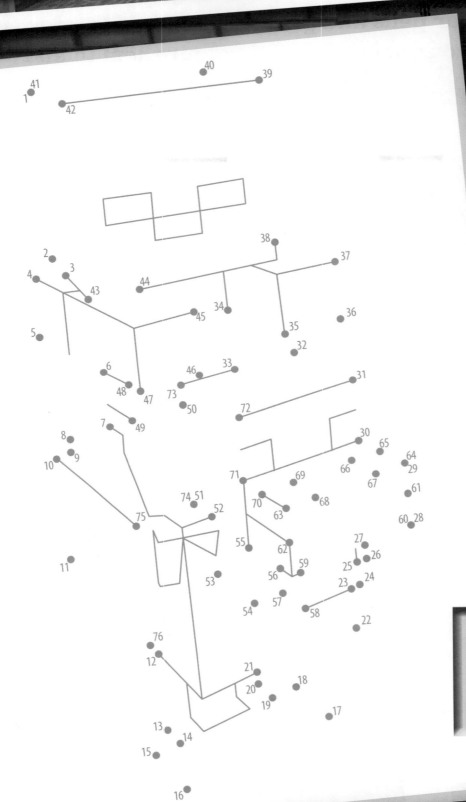

Join the dots
to complete
the picture...

16

PAGES PART 1

Spot The Difference

Can you spot six changes? Good luck!

Craftygrams

Rearrange the letters to name the mobs:

1. real pa bro 2. art bib 3. leg mows on 4. shrivel ifs 5. a cam bug me
6. need merit 7. check nick joey 8. neither elk tows 9. grand red one
10. dear rail nudge

11 CRAZIEST MINECRAFT

11 THE EYE

This beautifully designed map offers the perfect test of your jumping skills and sense of direction. You have to navigate your way to freedom through a surreal network of platforms winding up through the sky, all under the gaze of a giant eye wearing a top hat! It's certainly weird, but thoroughly absorbing. There are plenty of parkour maps to choose from in Minecraft, but the sheer imagination in The Eye makes it one of our absolute favourites.

tinyurl.com/MCAnnual2018Build11

10 CYBORG PENGUIN

Proof that your only real limit in Minecraft is your own imagination (and spare time), here's a giant emperor penguin. But it's not just any giant emperor penguin – it has dragon wings, bandages (because it's also an Egyptian mummy), and half a metal face (because it's also a cyborg). Oh, and Minecraft user rosedragon has given it a jetpack too. Nice touch!

tinyurl.com/MCAnnual2018Build10

9 UNDERWATER CITY

Where most cities in Minecraft consist of tall, chunky blocks, Lumina Nocturnale is an inviting collection of sweeping curves and circles. All cool greys, minimal interiors and acres of glass,

BUILDS

MINECRAFT
EASTER EGG & BUNNY

8 TNT EASTER EGG AND BUNNY

Having a bad day? Then maybe watching a colossal statue of an Easter bunny explode will put a smile on your face – it certainly worked for us! The bunny and its accompanying egg are made almost entirely from TNT blocks, and detonating the thing is satisfyingly messy. Just make sure you're standing at a safe distance in Survival mode.

tinyurl.com/MCAnnual2018Build8

7 THE TEMPLE OF NOTCH

Here's a very strange build that pays homage to Markus "Notch" Persson, the creator of Minecraft. Having placed an offering in the Well of Destiny, a pair of doors open and you're confronted with a gigantic replica of Notch's bearded face. Depending on your luck, the statue's eyes will open and you'll either be showered with diamonds and gold or, more disturbingly, the floor will fall away and you'll drop into a pit of lava...

tinyurl.com/MCAnnual2018Build7

this is truly a city from the future, and what's more, it's absolutely huge! That most of the build is located underwater just makes it all the more impressive.

tinyurl.com/MCAnnual2018Build9

5 WOLF WITH TOP HAT

These days, the only people who wear top hats are posh people and magicians. But if this build is to be believed, top hats are also fashionable among wolves. To be fair, the headgear really suits this chap's face, though he does wear an expression that says, "You'd better not be laughing at my hat!"

tinyurl.com/MCAnnual2018Build5

6 ANIMAL CANNON

We're not sure how useful this is, but it looks like a lot of fun to play around with. YouTube user Kiershar has created his own animal cannon, which is capable of flinging a pig so far that it can never be found. The ingenious design uses a tower packed full of TNT to launch an animal in a minecart clear across the game map. "Pig and the minecarts were never seen again," Kiershar wrote after a test launch. "I have walked for a few Minecraft days in the direction of the launch, with no success. It's time to call off the search. RIP Pig."

tinyurl.com/MCAnnual2018Build6

4 GRABBER MACHINE

This build is a simulation of one of those grabber machines where you try (and generally fail) to pick up a stuffed toy with a wobbly metal claw. But because this is Minecraft, you control the grabber by stepping on a set of pressure plates, and the items inside the machine include creepers, witches and ocelots. Okay, so they aren't great prizes, but at least Seth's machine doesn't eat up all your spare change!

tinyurl.com/MCAnnual2018Build4

3 AUTOMATED CHICKEN FARM

Creating a plentiful, reliable source of food is one of the keys to survival in Minecraft. But what if you freed up time you'd otherwise spend harvesting food by creating your own automated chicken farm? A player calling himself Data has done exactly this – he's built a huge facility where caged chickens lay eggs, which hatch into chicks. These are then cooked with lava blocks when they're fully grown. Disturbing, but useful – and very tasty!

tinyurl.com/MCAnnual2018Build3

2 SHARK SUBMARINE

Movies like *Jaws* may portray great white sharks as villains but, let's face it, we all know they also look brilliant! They're fast, toothsome, and have a big, pointy dorsal fin that looks like a spoiler on a sports car. So what better way to live at sea than in a huge submarine shaped like a shark? This build is nicely appointed with a dining room, officer's quarters and sick bay, while you'll also find anti-aircraft guns and torpedo launchers – perfect for fending off shark hunters!

tinyurl.com/MCAnnual2018Build2

1 SELF-BUILDING CASTLE

Now this really is crazy! Pressing a button causes an entire castle to rise up out of the desert, as though it's being built before your very eyes. It's all powered by redstone – plus about 25,000 pistons – but the sheer brilliance of its design is beyond anything we've seen in Minecraft before. Jaw-dropping? If we didn't know better, we'd say it was magic!

tinyurl.com/MCAnnual2018Build1

35
It's always worth adding extra lighting to a village to keep mobs away. You could even build a defensive wall around it if you want to keep the villagers safe!

36
Elytra can't be crafted, but you can repair them using leather on an anvil. Four leather will completely repair one set of elytra.

37
Don't repair any enchanted items on a crafting grid, otherwise you'll lose the enchantments. Use an anvil and raw materials instead.

38
Crafting minecart rails takes up a lot of resources and time, so when you stumble across an abandoned mine be sure to take as many of the unused rails as you can carry back to the surface with you.

A defensive wall

Be careful what you repair on an anvil

Don't anger a wolf!

39
Don't bother killing baby animals when you come across them. They don't drop anything – not even experience – when they die, so there's no reason to waste your weapons on them. Wait until they're fully grown.

40
Wolf packs will actively hunt other animals, but they'll leave you alone unless you injure them. Hurt one and the whole pack will come for you though, so take care!

41
Rather than dyeing wool, find a sheep and dye it. This permanently changes the wool colour even after the wool regrows, so you can keep shearing your sheep for an unending supply of coloured wool.

Chickens will follow seed

Don't eliminate whole herds

Horses can heal by eating hay

42 Most animals will follow you if you hold a certain type of food. For chickens it's grain, for rabbits and pigs it's carrots, and so on. Use this behaviour to lead lots of animals at once so you can pen them in.

43 Always leave at least two animals in a herd alive so that you can breed more if you need to. Killing the whole herd is fine in the short term, but you'll regret it when you need the resources later!

44 If you walk too far from a tamed wolf it teleports next to you, so don't worry about losing it during a fight!

45 Horses, donkeys and mules can eat hay bales, healing up to 10 hearts. They're by far the most efficient way to restore your ride's health, so make sure you keep a few near your bases.

46 Feeding sugar to a horse has a variety of effects. It heals adult horses, makes smaller ones grow faster and helps wild ones tame more easily.

47 The moon's phases affect how mobs spawn, so pay attention. Full moons are the most dangerous – you'll see more slimes and stronger mobs, possibly with enchanted weapons, so prepare for a big fight!

Full moons raise the chance of equipped mobs spawning

48 On harder modes, zombies will look for and try to break down wooden doors. Use steel doors activated by a button to keep them out – they can't ever break through metal.

49 You can tell what profession a zombie villager had when it was alive, and you can use that to help you decide whether to kill it or try curing it. They might make a useful trading partner!

50 Once you've built a portal, there's a small chance of zombie pigmen spawning near it, so make sure it's built somewhere out of the way, if not fenced in completely. You don't want any nasty surprises!

Huge mushrooms give lots of food

have them to hand whether you need unique decoration or a source of dyes.

51

Despite their short appearance, baby zombies are faster and more powerful than regular zombies, and can fit through smaller gaps, so take them out first! Otherwise, you might miss them while you're trying to fend off the larger ones!

52

It's hard to grow mushrooms, but if you use bone meal to turn them into huge mushrooms you can harvest up to two mushrooms per block, and an average huge mushroom will yield around 14 small ones. You'll never go hungry again!

53

Cocoa pods only grow naturally on jungle trees, but as soon as you find one you can farm pods on any tree trunk. It doesn't have to be part of a tree!

54

When you find a flower forest, stock up on rare plants you can't get anywhere else. That way you'll always

55

Large trees, like dark oak and jungle trees, can be grown by planting four saplings together then fertilising one with bone meal.

56

Cooked steak and pork chops are common food items that restore a lot of hunger points, so stock up on them, especially early in the game when you'll lose health quickly.

57

Save clownfish for taming ocelots. They have almost no other use and restore only a tiny amount of health if eaten, but will please ocelots as much as any other fish.

58

If you want to clear things like grass, flowers and ferns, drop a water source block so that it spreads in all directions, then pick it back up. The ground will be washed clean.

59

Remember that armour only protects you from physical attacks. Fire, fall damage and

Cocoa pods are found in jungle biomes

Stock up on dyes in a flower forest

Dark oaks can only be grown from four saplings

24

Armour doesn't protect you from everything

A shield with a pattern on it

drowning aren't any less dangerous, though you can apply enchantments to armour pieces which will make them that way.

60 You can repair rare chainmail armour by using iron ingots on an anvil. Chainmail armour is slightly weaker than iron armour, but holds better enchantments.

61 Enchant books, rather than items, then combine the book with the target tool/armour on an anvil. It costs more, but you won't end up with enchantments you don't like on your valuable equipment.

62 Use shears on cobwebs to cut them quickly.

63 Learn to use the most appropriate tool to break blocks. Wooden blocks usually break fastest with an axe, stone with a pickaxe, and dirt with a spade.

64 Place your favourite type of arrow in your offhand inventory slot and your bow will prioritise those arrows. Otherwise, it takes them from the lowest numbered inventory slot.

65 You can combine a banner with a shield to transfer the pattern onto it. You can't remove the pattern or apply a new one though, so make sure you do it right!

66 Shields can't be enchanted directly, but you can apply Unbreaking to it by using an anvil and enchanted book.

67 When fighting the wither, create a distraction by building lots of golems. They can't do much to hurt the wither themselves, but it will attack anything it sees, and that will give you more time to attack it.

68 Destroy ender crystals with a bow and arrow while the ender dragon is healing itself with them and you'll deal a lot of damage.

CONTINUED ON P34

Rare chainmail armour

BEAT EVERY MOB

There are loads of different enemies in Minecraft, so knowing how to beat them all is essential! Here are the best tactics for every hostile mob!

BLAZE

Use a bow and arrow to hit blazes while they're in the air, and carry a shield to block their fireballs. Eating an enchanted golden apple gives you five minutes of Fire Resistance, so is useful to have when fighting blazes.

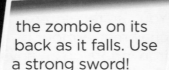
Blaze

CAVE SPIDER

Cave spider

They're weaker than regular spiders, but can poison you with a bite. Arrows from a Flame-enchanted bow should let you keep your distance, and if you miss they'll hopefully incinerate some of the cobwebs that stop you getting to the monster spawner they emerge from.

CHICKEN JOCKEY

The easiest way to kill a chicken jockey is to jump off a ledge, wait until it follows and is in mid-air, then attack

Chicken jockey

the zombie on its back as it falls. Use a strong sword!

CREEPER

A simple tactic: run forward, hit the creeper with your sword so that it's knocked backwards, then back away fast. It will either take damage and not blow up, or you'll be far enough away from the explosion that it doesn't damage you.

Creeper

ENDERMAN

The best way to fight endermen is to wear a pumpkin to get close without them teleporting away. Don't bother using ranged weapons as they'll teleport away before you get a chance. They also ignore tame wolves, so they're invaluable in a fight against one!

Enderman

ENDERMITE

They're weak, so a couple of strikes with a sword should do. Don't waste potions or other consumable items on them as they don't drop anything good.

Endermite

Evoker

Ghast

Magma cube

EVOKER

Shoot them with a bow and use your shield to block vex attacks. Try not to get too close until they're weak – the fang attacks are very strong but won't work if you're far away!

GHAST

With the longest range of any normal mob (over 100 blocks!), Ghasts can be hard to fight. You can hit their fireballs back at them to cause damage, which results in a very powerful explosion. The secret is to hide behind blocks when you're not attacking as they can't see through walls!

GUARDIAN & ELDER GUARDIAN

Fighting guardians is very difficult due to their strength, spikes, laser attacks and the fact that they live underwater.

Guardian

If you can wall them up and use a sponge to dry out the room that makes them easier to kill. Otherwise, get in close at one of their sides and hack away. Bring lots of enchanted armour and instant health potions!

MAGMA CUBE

Using a bow is the safest way to fight larger cubes, while smaller ones can be attacked with a sword. Never stay too close as magma cubes have double the attack rate of most mobs.

SHULKER

Wait for shulkers to open before attacking them – they're immune to arrows when they're closed, so don't waste any! Be careful if there are lots around – attack one shulker and others in the area will turn on you, so keep your back to the wall!

Shulker

Silverfish

Skeleton

Slime

SILVERFISH

Hurting one silverfish will cause others in the area to emerge and attack, unless you kill the silverfish in one hit. For this reason, the best way to fight them is with an enchanted/diamond sword, to help avoid a swarm.

SKELETON

When fighting skeletons, use a shield to block their arrows then attack between shots with a sword or bow. If you don't have a shield, circle the skeleton while attacking and it should be unable to target you long enough to get an arrow on target!

SKELETON HORSEMAN

There's no great trick to killing horsemen – use projectiles and/or a bow and arrow to hit them – but if you attack and kill the rider you'll be able to take the horse for yourself.

SLIME

Large slimes split into smaller ones, so tackle them as they appear, otherwise you'll get overwhelmed. Always start by killing the smallest slime first. If you're fighting in a swamp, luring them into water is a great way to slow them down.

SPIDER

The best way to kill normal spiders is to wait until they chase you, then walk backwards while swinging your sword. When they jump at you they'll be hurt and knocked back, then be far enough away to try jumping again.

SPIDER JOCKEY

When fighting a spider jockey, attack the skeleton first. Spider jockeys are rare but very dangerous because both the spider and skeleton can attack you. The best way to deal with them is to focus on the skeleton as it's more dangerous.

Skeleton horseman

Spider

Spider jockey

Vindicator

Witch

Wolf

VINDICATOR

Don't use a shield as their axes will disable it! Instead, use a splash Potion of Slowness to keep them in place, then hit them fast and often with your sword!

WITCH

Witches use potions to heal themselves and weaken you, so keep a bucket of milk to cure yourself. Use weapons that continue to inflict damage like fire, poison arrows/potions and lava to counteract their healing. Don't stop for a second, or they'll return to full strength!

WITHER SKELETON

The wither effect can be very dangerous and can even kill you, so don't let a wither skeleton near you. Use a bow and arrow to attack them, and throw splash Potions of Healing. Wither skeletons

have swords not bows, so if you keep your distance you should be safe.

WOLF

A pack of wolves will only attack if you provoke them first, so don't hurt them, but if you do the best protection is to get up high, usually in a tree. Don't try and fight them all at once!

ZOMBIE/ZOMBIE VILLAGER

Zombies are the easiest mobs to kill because they're slow and weak. Stick to using a basic sword – save stronger weapons for stronger mobs. If you're attacked by multiple zombies at once, a splash Potion of Healing can harm several in one go.

ZOMBIE PIGMAN

Because they carry swords, zombie pigmen can do a lot of damage. The best way to fight them is to climb on a two-block pillar then strike downwards. The pigmen will surround the pillar but be unable to climb it, so you can pick them off from above.

Wither skeleton

Zombie villager

Zombie pigman

PUZZLE

Blockdoku

Can you colour in the grid of blocks following these rules?
- Each small square must contain a coloured block
- Each of the brown rectangles must contain all SIX types of block
- No block type can appear on any line twice, horizontally or vertically...

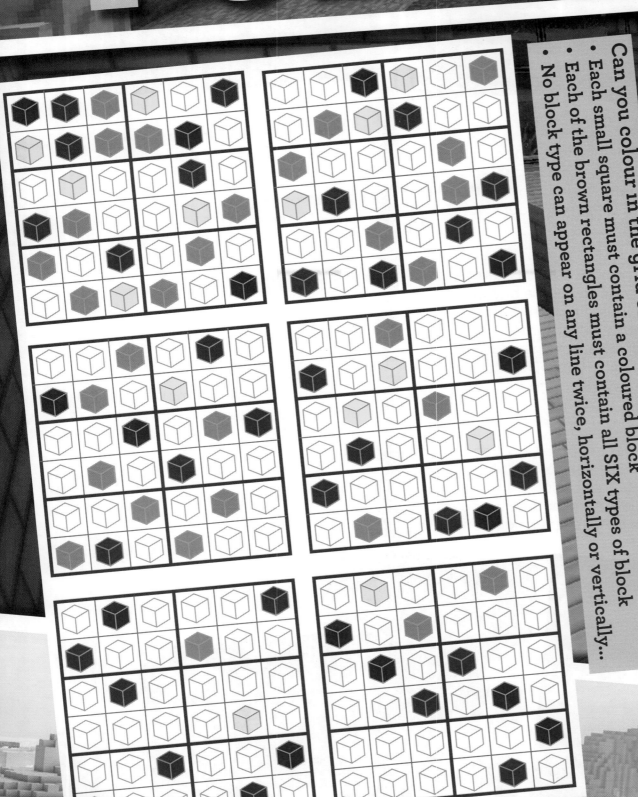

30

PAGES

Super Sword Maze

Think you've got what it takes to plunder the pearl from our massive sword-shaped maze? Well, maybe you do... Just make sure you have plenty of supplies before you go in!

Start>>>

5 AMAZING POTIONS

There are LOADS of good potions

Smashing bottles o' enchanting releases experience orbs

Potions are cool ways you can boost your abilities, heal damage you've taken, or even cause damage to mobs. There are tonnes of different recipes, all with different effects and uses. Here, we look at some of the rarer potions that you might not know about!

For each potion, we give you the quickest recipe to create it – brew the ingredients into a water bottle in the order they're listed. Remember you may need blaze powder to power the reaction too!

BOTTLE O' ENCHANTING
Recipe: Can only be traded
This potion can be bought off cleric villagers if you trade with them enough to reach their highest trading levels. It costs between three and 11 emeralds. They can be thrown like splash potions and will drop experience orbs with 3-11 points. They're available in all editions, but at the time of writing trading isn't available in Pocket Edition, so they're only available in the creative inventory!
TIP: Don't just use these immediately — store them until you actually need them. Otherwise, if you die, you've wasted those emeralds!

POTION OF WATER BREATHING (EXTENDED)
Recipe: Nether wart, pufferfish, redstone
If you have to go on a long boat ride, it's worth keeping a Potion of Water Breathing with you because it means you can survive underwater. While the potion is active, your oxygen bar won't deplete. A standard one lasts for three minutes, but add redstone and it will last for eight.
TIP: The potion also slightly improves your ability to see underwater!

Water Breathing improves underwater vision too

Healing potions hurt the undead

POTION OF HEALING (LEVEL II)

Recipe: Nether wart, glistering melon, glowstone

The Level II Potion of Healing is the quickest way you can heal yourself (or most other mobs) because it instantly gives 8 points of health (4 hearts) when you drink it!

TIP: Add gunpowder to turn it into a splash potion – it will harm undead mobs like skeletons and zombies.

POTION OF LUCK

Recipe: Uncraftable!

The Potion of Luck can't be brewed, but is available in the PC and Console Editions inside the creative inventory. Drinking the potion increases the player's "luck" attribute by one point for five minutes. This means any treasure chests that are first opened while the potion effect is active are more likely to have rare or high-level loot in them.

TIP: To get the most out of the potion, drink it then fish for the entire duration of the potion's effect as fishing loot is also affected by luck.

POTION OF DECAY

Recipe: Uncraftable!

The Potion of Decay can't be brewed, but it's available in Pocket Edition if you use Creative mode. It inflicts the wither effect, which causes one point of damage every second (half of one heart) and lasts for 40 seconds. This means it can cause up to 40 points (20 hearts) of damage in a single use.

Unlike some health-sapping effects, a Potion of Decay is capable of killing you, so try and drink milk to cure it as quickly as possible!

TIP: It's best used as a splash or lingering potion – it's not like you want to drink this one yourself!

The Potion of Decay inflicts the wither effect

101 MINECRAFT TRICKS PART 3

69 If villagers get injured by mob attacks, you can heal them by using a splash/lingering Potion of Healing or by trading an item with them. It's faster than waiting for a new villager to spawn and/or grow to adulthood!

70 Monster spawners are rare and can be really tricky to find, but destroying one gets you more immediate experience than anything else in the game. Well, other than killing a boss creature!

71 It can be useful to carry a bed with you when exploring the Overworld so that you can wall yourself up and skip nights. Just be careful to stay alive. If the last bed you slept in doesn't exist, you get sent back to the world's spawn point.

Mob spawners are rare

Take a shortcut through the Nether

You can walk on lilypads

72 Never try to carry too much when you're exploring underground. Use chests to create small temporary storage areas. Otherwise, if you die before you make it back to base, you'll lose everything!

73 You can build shortcuts through the Nether to travel long distances and save time!. Every step you take in the Nether is equivalent to eight steps in the Overworld, so journey times are massively shortened, though it's obviously a lot riskier!

74 You can walk on lilypads while they're floating, so they're a great way to get out of the water for a bit or make simple bridges.

Remember to pull up the carpet in igloos

An exposed diamond vein

Watch out for silverfish

75 Boats are faster than walking, so if you're travelling or exploring a new area, sticking to water will allow you to cover more ground than clambering over uneven terrain.

76 Remember to pull up the carpet in igloos to see if they've generated a basement. Only 50% of igloos have basements, though!

77 Diamond ore veins can generate diagonally, so break all of the blocks around any piece of ore you find to make sure you don't miss this valuable block.

Soul sand can trap players and mobs

78 If you're in extreme hills, a stronghold or an igloo basement, watch out for monster egg blocks. They look normal, but break a little slower than you expect and release silverfish when they're finally destroyed.

79 If you encounter a dead end while exploring, you might want to block it off with a bar of cobblestone so that you don't accidentally go down there again. Place a torch on the front so that if you ever encounter it from the other side, you know where you blocked it off from.

80 It's quicker to discover diamonds in caves than it is to mine for them. They usually appear near underground lava lakes, so follow the edges of those and you should then find some diamonds quite easily.

81 If you need to blow up some TNT, don't just set it on fire with a flint and steel then run. Use redstone dust to create a "fuse" and activate it from a safe distance with a redstone charge (i.e. a redstone torch).

82 Soul sand makes mobs (and players) stick to it, so you can trap them by surrounding soul sand with slabs that let them in easily, but stop them stepping out.

83 Using a nametag on a mob prevents it from despawning, though it's still possible for it to die. If the mob is hostile, it will also disappear if you set the difficulty to Peaceful, so don't be surprised if you do that.

You get one gateway per dragon kill

see what's around them. The location is marked by a green blob.

84 Soul sand will suffocate silverfish and endermites, causing them to die. You can use this knowledge to trap silverfish in strongholds.

85 You can submerge yourself in water to largely escape the effects of TNT or a creeper explosion – they'll barely touch you!

86 End gateways only generate when you kill an ender dragon. You can use them to teleport around the End by throwing ender pearls into them. Every ender dragon you kill generates a new End gateway, and when you travel through one it generates an exit gateway so you can get back.

87 Make a map of your base area and place it on the wall in an item frame so that any visitors to your world can easily

88 You don't have to put coal in furnaces. Almost anything wooden can burn, including saplings, so it's a useful way of getting rid of junk and hanging onto valuable coal.

89 If you want to collect lots of snow, build a snow golem in a small pit or dark room (making sure it doesn't get too hot!) and it will generate a layer of snow as it wanders around, which you can easily harvest.

90 Incinerators are useful for getting rid of blocks, but fire and lava can cause severe damage to you and your base. A cactus block, however, will destroy items that touch it but can't set anything on fire, so it's a lot safer!

91 You can cast fishing rods onto pressure plates to set them off from a distance.

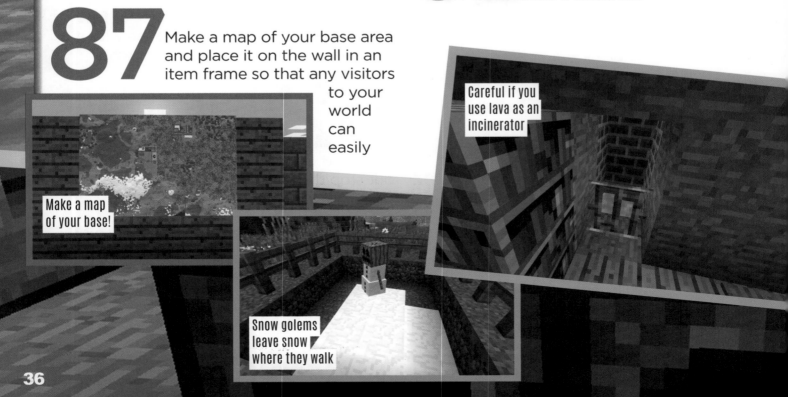

Make a map of your base!

Careful if you use lava as an incinerator

Snow golems leave snow where they walk

Netherbrick fences are more efficient

You can wash off dye in cauldrons

Leather Tunic

92
If you're making fences, remember that six Nether bricks will create six Nether brick fences, whereas six sticks will create only two wooden fences.

93
Don't use glass blocks as windows. Six glass blocks make 16 glass panes, so you cover more space using them!

94
Netherbrick fences don't join up to wooden fences, so you can use a Netherbrick fencepost to create a gate that lets you through but keeps animals penned in.

95
Cauldrons can be filled with water and used to wash the dye off leather clothing, or fill three glass bottles.

96
You can expand villages by building shelters with doors. Each new door increases the chance of a new villager spawning.

97
You can force most trees to always grow tall by planting the saplings in holes three blocks deep.

98
Beacons can be built overlapping to save resources, as long as the beacon blocks at the top are at least a block apart.

99
Destroy the pressure plate in desert temples as soon as you find them, otherwise a mob might spawn and set off the TNT!

100
You can build an End portal in Creative. Just make sure the portal blocks are all facing the right way (with the lines pointing inwards), otherwise it won't activate properly!

101
Polar bear cubs spawn naturally, but there's no way to breed polar bears, so don't try!

Glass panes are more efficient windows than blocks

You can't breed polar bears

39

END! 41

5 AMAZING RECIPES

Minecraft has loads of recipes, some of which you use all the time, and some of which you might never realise you can make. There are some super cool, rare and useful items in the game that are almost impossible to find but can be crafted easily – as long as you know what you need and how to get it!

To help you along, here are five amazing recipes you might want to try out.

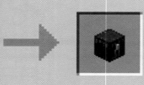

An ender chest can't be looted

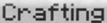

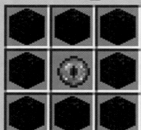

ENDER CHEST

Use a crafting table to surround one eye of ender with eight obsidian blocks, and you create an ender chest. Every ender chest you build leads to the same storage area, so you can use them to store useful items you might want to access from lots of different places.

TIP: Every player has their own ender chest storage area, even when using the same chests, so you can use them to hide items from other players who might steal them!

ARMOUR STAND

Created from six sticks and a stone slab, armour stands can be used to display armour. They don't appear anywhere in the game, so you might not realise you can craft them, but you can!

They're mostly just for decoration, but you can use them to group suits of armour for easy access.

TIP: You can put mob heads and pumpkins on top of armour stands instead of helmets and caps, so you can use them to create little scarecrows or statues!

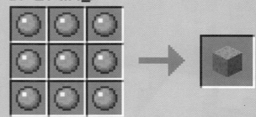

Turn an armour stand into a scarecrow!

on one you don't take any damage and bounce back up instead!

TIP: Water flowing over slime blocks will push items faster than water flowing over normal blocks, so they're good for transporting things!

FIRE CHARGE

Craft blaze powder, coal (or charcoal) and gunpowder together and you create three fire charges. You can't shoot them out of your hand, but you can put them in dispensers. When the dispenser is activated, it will shoot a fireball. They're also an ingredient in firework stars, allowing you to make fireworks!

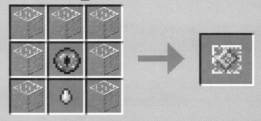

END CRYSTAL

To make an End crystal, you need one eye of ender, one ghast tear and seven glass blocks. They're only generated in the End where they heal the ender dragon, and can't be collected.

   If you've killed the ender dragon, you can use End crystals to summon a new one by placing one on each side of the exit portal in the End. They can only be placed on obsidian or bedrock blocks.

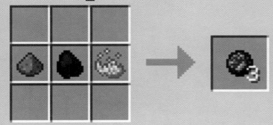

TIP: You can use a fire charge to light a fire by "using" it on a block or mob in front of you, though it will use up the charge and could set you on fire too!

TIP: End crystals explode when destroyed, so while they look cool, don't put them near anything valuable!

SLIME BLOCK

When you kill a slime, you can collect slimeballs, which can be crafted as part of leads, magma cream and sticky pistons. You can also craft together nine slimeballs to make a slime block. They slow down mobs and players, but if you jump

Slime blocks let you bounce!

Crystals can resurrect the dragon

43

AMAZING ENCHANT

Enchantments are one of the most fun things in Minecraft, because they give your items special abilities!

Enchantments can be applied to two groups of items or tools. Primary items can generate the enchantment spontaneously by being enchanted on an enchantment table. Secondary items can hold the enchantment, but only if combined with an enchanted book using an anvil.

Treasure enchantments are found only on enchanted books that appear in chests when fishing or when trading. At the time of writing, they're only in the PC and console editions, but will soon be added to the Pocket Edition!

UNBREAKING

Most items in Minecraft eventually fall apart through wear or damage, which makes Unbreaking invaluable.

Items enchanted with Unbreaking last several times longer than unenchanted ones. Level I Unbreaking makes items last roughly twice as long, while Level III Unbreaking makes them last four times as long.

Primary: Pickaxe, shovel, axe, sword, bow, fishing rod, helmet, chestplate, leggings, boots
Secondary: Hoe, shears, flint and steel, carrot on a stick, shield and elytra
TIP: Enchant diamond items – you get the most value from the enchantment that way!

Most enchantments can be applied like this

Unbreaking makes diamond items last almost forever!

FROST WALKER

This treasure enchantment can be applied only to boots, and allows the player to walk on water. At Level I, any water blocks within a three-block radius will be turned into ice. At Level II, the radius expands to four blocks. At both levels, it prevents the player taking damage if they walk over magma blocks.

Note that it can't be combined with the Depth Strider enchantment!
Primary: None
Secondary: Boots
TIP: Wear Frost Walker-enchanted boots when you visit the Nether!

MENTS

Frost Walker is a fun enchantment for boots

The Curse of Binding means you're stuck with what you're wearing!

Curse of Vanishing will stop them – or you – getting hold of it after you die.

CURSE OF BINDING

The Curse of Binding is a treasure enchantment that has only one level and can be applied to most wearable items.

Any item with the Curse of Binding is impossible to remove once the player wears it. The item can still break, and will fall off when the player dies, but once you put it on it stays on!

Primary: None

Secondary: Helmet, chestplate, leggings, boots, elytra, pumpkin, mob heads

TIP: Put cursed and weak items in a dispenser, and you can automatically equip them to people as a trap.

CURSE OF VANISHING

Another treasure enchantment, the Curse of Vanishing is a one-level enchantment that makes sure an item disappears as soon as the player dies, rather than getting dropped like a normal inventory item.

Primary: None

Secondary: Pickaxe, shovel, axe, fishing rod, helmet, chestplate, leggings, boots, sword, bow, hoe, shears, flint and steel, carrot on a stick, shield, elytra, pumpkin, mob heads

TIP: If you have a powerful weapon and don't want it to fall into enemy hands, the

LUCK OF THE SEA

If you want to make yourself more likely to get the rare treasure enchantments, it's worth using the Luck of the Sea enchantment. This lowers the chance of catching junk and fish when you fish, and raises the chance of catching treasure, including enchanted books!

Primary: Fishing rod

Secondary: None

TIP: Combine with the Lure enchantment, which makes the rate of catches increase by up to 50% when fishing.

Items with Vanishing won't drop when you die

45

10 TIPS FOR A BETTER BUILD

Want to make your creations in Minecraft look cooler than ever? Here are some tips to help you create better buildings!

1 LAY SLABS

If you have to create a large floor space, don't waste time digging up the ground and then laying blocks in it – just use slabs instead. Slabs double the area you can cover with your resources (i.e. three wood planks makes six slabs) and can easily be turned into steps that let the player walk up.

2 PLAN BEFORE YOU BUILD

To make sure your building looks good before you actually make it, why not plan your foundations first? You don't have to do this on paper – it can be as simple as building a wall plan on the ground before you start.

Lay slabs

Plan first

Stick to a theme

A sloped roof creates an attic inside!

3 PICK A THEME AND STICK TO IT

The best buildings look like they were made using the same kind of materials. If you want to build a castle, make sure your walls are built entirely out of stone-type blocks. If you're building a woodland hut, use only wood.

4 ADD A SLOPED ROOF

Sloped roofs look professional and give you the added bonus of creating an attic space inside! Stair blocks are useful for creating a sloped roof that's

Double doors look better than single ones

Experiment with windows

Make your buildings L-shaped

allows you to split up the interior into different rooms and create interesting spaces on multiple levels. You could even have the top floor overhang the bottom one, like a Tudor house!

8 BUILD PATHS

It always looks good to run a path between things you've built. It will help you (and other people) remember where to go. Stone of some kind is usually your best choice. Try simple stone and/or stone slabs, though gravel is also a fun alternative because it makes a nice crunching sound when you walk over it.

also tall enough not to look stupid. Make sure it overhangs your walls slightly too!

5 PLACE DOUBLE DOORS

Double doors make it clear where the main entrance to your building is, and give an appearance of grandeur and scale that a single door can't. Try to pick the right kind of door – each type of wood creates a different looking one.

6 TRY OUT DIFFERENT WINDOWS

Windows are essential in any build, but that doesn't mean they have to be the same every time. Experiment with using different colours of glass, or blocks instead of panes. See what different effects you can achieve by combining different types!

7 DON'T MAKE ALL OF YOUR BUILDINGS INTO BOXES

In real life, houses are rarely just featureless cubes, and it's actually quite common for houses to be L-shaped. This

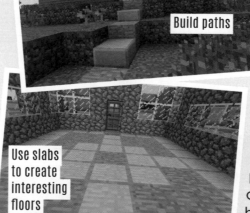

Build paths

Use slabs to create interesting floors

Automate your doors

9 DESIGN INTERESTING FLOORS

Whether you're using tiles, stone or carpet, making a design on your floor will improve an otherwise empty room. Tile symmetrical patterns for the best look, though you could also make pixel art if you're feeling creative. You'll be surprised at how much better it makes a room feel!

10 AUTOMATE DOORS

Put pressure plates in front of doors so they open and close automatically: when you approach a door it opens, and when you're through it closes. Just don't put them on the outside of your house, because zombies and other mobs can trigger them too!

EPIC MINECRAFT YOUTUBERS

Lots of people first heard about Minecraft by watching one of the thousands upon thousands of YouTube videos about the game. Here are some of our favourite YouTubers. Check them out if you haven't already!

SQAISHEY QUACK
www.youtube.com/user/sqaishey
What could be more fun than following the adventures of a yellow duck playing Minecraft?! Not many things. Sqaishey Duck is aimed at younger players, with a new video most days, including lots and lots of minigames!

Sqaishey Quack

LDSHADOWLADY
www.youtube.com/user/ldshadowlady
A channel that uses lots of mods to play Minecraft! Lizzie, the host, covers loads of other games too, and she loves Minecraft minigames!

LDShadowLady

BIONICMC
www.youtube.com/user/ItsBionicYT
If you've never seen the SkyWars and Factions mods for Minecraft before, BionicMC's YouTube channel is a great place to find out all about them! Follow the assorted battles here, and check out some of the mob grinder builds too!

BionicMC

THE ATLANTIC CRAFT
www.youtube.com/user/TheAtlanticCraft
If you're looking for something a little more advanced, some of the videos you'll find at TheAtlanticCraft are just the ticket. They're hosted by TheCodyMaverick and JoeBuzz, and when you're done with their Minecraft

TheAtlanticCraft

DanTDM

work, check out their *Frozen* parody video, "Let It Glow"!

JEROMEASF
www.youtube.com/user/JeromeASF
You might want to get yourself a drink before you settle down to watch one of Jerome's videos as they tend to be on the long side. But then he's got so much stuff to get through, and he's a great way to get to know some epic mods for the game!

JeromeASF

POPULARMMOS
www.youtube.com/user/popularMMOs
You'll find some amazing stuff here, with brilliant Let's Play videos, mob and arena battles, and generally two new videos going up every day! You're bound to find something you like and, chances are, quite a lot!

PopularMMOs

THE DIAMOND MINECART
www.youtube.com/user/ TheDiamondMinecart
For good reason, DanTDM is one of the most famous Minecrafters on the planet, and his YouTube channel has tons of Minecraft stuff on it (although he's also distracted by lots of other games!). You'll learn a lot watching The Diamond Minecart, and his videos are really good fun too!

STAMPY
www.youtube.com/user/ stampylonghead
Probably the most well known Minecrafter on the planet, Stampy's YouTube channel is bursting with videos, with a new one added every day. His Let's Play videos are brilliant, and he's always looking for new series and ideas! No wonder millions of people subscribe!

19 blocks left
Stampy

THE DEFINITIVE WORLD SEED

Seeds generate Minecraft's worlds

There are weird things to find...

...and cool sights to see!

WHAT ARE SEEDS?

Every one of Minecraft's infinite worlds has a world seed powering it. These are small strings of letters and numbers, and they're used to power the complicated algorithms that allow Minecraft to create its landscapes without storing tonnes of data. That's why you can download the game to your phone, tablet or PC without it taking ages!

WHAT ELSE DO THEY DO?

World seeds have another huge benefit: you can share them with other people so they can generate the same world. If you find something cool, sharing the seed lets other people see it too!

Each one is unique and special

HOW CAN I SHARE MY SEED?

World seeds can only be shared across versions that use the same algorithm, so Pocket, Console and PC editions can't use the same seeds. But if you're using the same edition as someone else, it's easy to generate the world they're in. Just enter the world seed in the advanced options when you create a new world.

HOW DO I FIND THE SEED I'M USING?

Every world you generate has a seed. To find the seed of the world you're currently in, type "/seed" into the console on the PC edition, or look on the World Options screen in Pocket Edition.

HOW MANY SEEDS ARE THERE?

On the PC, there are a total of 18,446,744,073,709,551,616 (18 quintillion!) seeds, each leading to its own unique world. Console, Pocket and Windows 10 editions have just 4 billion...!

GUIDE

Seed bigmountain

Seed 0

Seed -3500229128833691836

PC EDITION SEEDS

These seeds were all tested on version 1.11.2, but they should work on other versions too!

Seed: 0

Start near a massive desert with a large village that crosses into a grassy biome! Very rare. If you explore past the village, you can also find a desert temple and a savanna plateau with horses!

Seed: bigmountain

Starts you near a huge mountain range, overlooking a big flower forest! There are loads of biomes in this area, so it's a good place to start if you like seeing some really diverse things quickly.

Seed: -4589128118707775879

Woodland mansions can be tough to find, but this seed spawns you close to one! Walk in the direction you're facing when you spawn and you'll soon see it appear on the horizon.

Seed: -3500229128833691836

Want to check out some cold biomes? This seed starts you near a selection of cold taiga, ice plains and ice spikes biomes, and you'll be able to see polar bears and igloos, as well as fight strays without going very far!

Seed: 1461928132

This seed starts you next to what is probably the game's rarest biome – the mesa (bryce) desert – which has tall clay pillars, orange sand, and surface-level mineshafts!

Seed: -6980839137331707558

When you spawn, turn around and walk in the opposite direction, and you'll come to a place where a savanna meets a desert. On the left is a rare savanna village. On the right is a desert village with a ravine by it, and if you explore the ravine you'll find an incredibly rare fossil (at X:113 Z:-141)!

Seed -4589128118707775879

Seed 1461928132

51

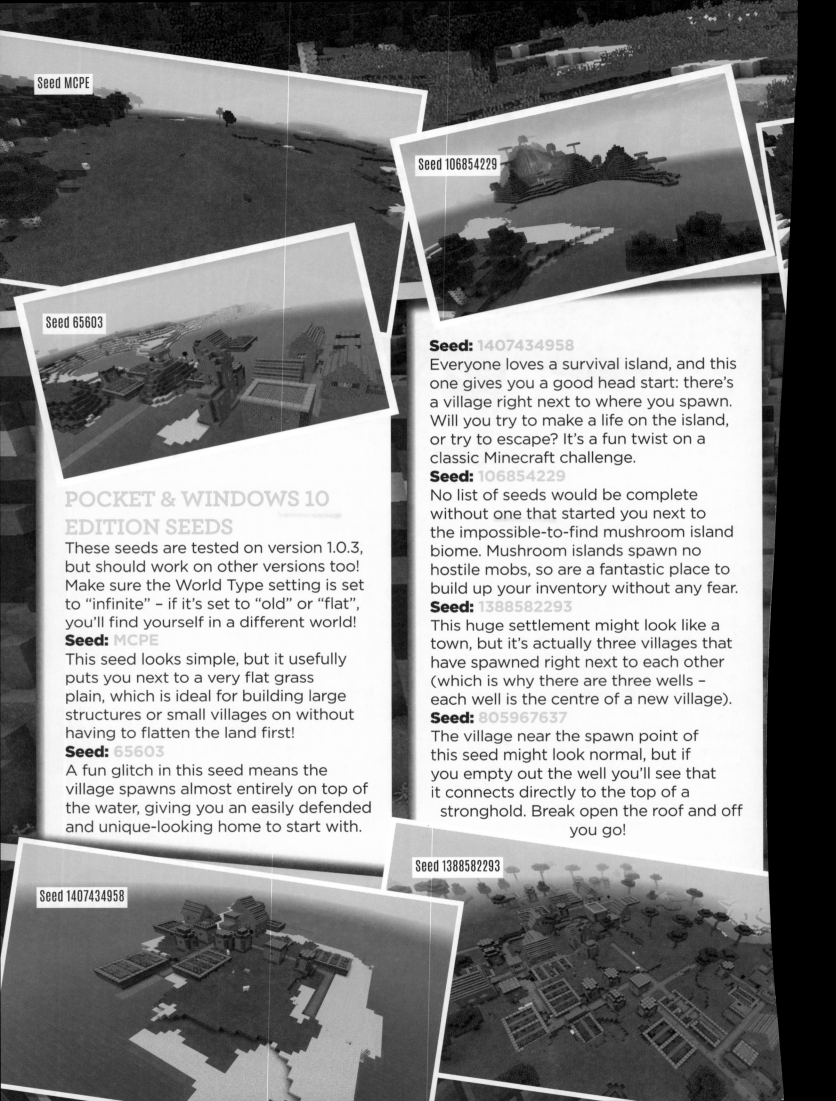

Seed MCPE

Seed 106854229

Seed 65603

POCKET & WINDOWS 10 EDITION SEEDS

These seeds are tested on version 1.0.3, but should work on other versions too! Make sure the World Type setting is set to "infinite" – if it's set to "old" or "flat", you'll find yourself in a different world!

Seed: MCPE

This seed looks simple, but it usefully puts you next to a very flat grass plain, which is ideal for building large structures or small villages on without having to flatten the land first!

Seed: 65603

A fun glitch in this seed means the village spawns almost entirely on top of the water, giving you an easily defended and unique-looking home to start with.

Seed: 1407434958

Everyone loves a survival island, and this one gives you a good head start: there's a village right next to where you spawn. Will you try to make a life on the island, or try to escape? It's a fun twist on a classic Minecraft challenge.

Seed: 106854229

No list of seeds would be complete without one that started you next to the impossible-to-find mushroom island biome. Mushroom islands spawn no hostile mobs, so are a fantastic place to build up your inventory without any fear.

Seed: 1388582293

This huge settlement might look like a town, but it's actually three villages that have spawned right next to each other (which is why there are three wells – each well is the centre of a new village).

Seed: 805967637

The village near the spawn point of this seed might look normal, but if you empty out the well you'll see that it connects directly to the top of a stronghold. Break open the roof and off you go!

Seed 1388582293

Seed 1407434958

Seed -126880078651571709

Seed 547195040906608474

CONSOLE EDITION SEEDS

All of the seeds listed below were tested and verified as working on the latest console versions we had access to: TU48 (Xbox 360), CU38 (Xbox One), PS3/PS4/PS Vita 1.41 and Wii U Patch 17. They should work on later versions too though!

Seed: -126880078651571709
Ever seen extreme temperatures side by side? This seed spawns you right next to a jungle biome, which is immediately connected to a cold taiga biome. Very strange!

Seed: -289973135
Survival island challenges are a great way to spend time on the Console Edition, and this is a pretty cool one! You start on a long island covered in trees, with plenty of resources and terrain to explore. It's a great place to get started!

Seed: -471883715052553104
You'll spawn near a desert, which has a desert village containing a blacksmiths, so you can get your hands

on some awesome free loot. Then explore the nearby cave system to find a stronghold with a working End portal!

Seed: 547195040906608474
Start near two of Minecraft's rarest features: an ocean monument and a mesa biome! Ideal for exploring things you might not have encountered before.

Seed: 5079366387731216932
If you're looking for igloos, look no further than this seed, which starts you not far from an ice spikes biome, which contains at least one igloo. There are also three villages and a desert temple within close distance, so you'll have a lot to find!

Seed: -671258039
If you hate looking around for diamonds, this spawn is a good place to start as the nearby village contains no fewer than NINE, meaning you can make a set of diamond tools or some pieces of diamond armour virtually as soon as you start the game!

Seed -289973135

Seed -671258039

AMAZING MINECRAFT RECORDS

While some of these may have been beaten by the time you read this, here are some formidable challenges for those of you who want to be the world's best at Minecraft! These records have all been verified by the *Guinness Book of Records*.

> LONGEST MINECRAFT GAMING MARATHON

Martin Fornleitner, who spent – get this! – 24 hours and 10 minutes playing the game back in 2011. Yikes!

> LONGEST TUNNEL IN MINECRAFT

In 2013, Lachlan Etherton of Australia built an incredible tunnel that ran for 10,502 blocks and took 10 minutes just to walk through! Since then, in March 2017, someone even beat that.

ItzEpicGeorge built a 100,000-block tunnel that at game walking speed takes over six hours to get through!

> LONGEST MINECRAFT JOURNEY

You can keep walking for ever and ever if you really want to in Minecraft, and Kurt J Mac must have felt he was doing just that when he started exploring the Far Lands (which were removed from the game in version 1.8, but Kurt keeps an old version running). He had walked over 2000 km in the game as of 2015, and you can follow his ongoing efforts at **farlandsorbust.com**

Stone Titans: largest pyramid built in Minecraft

Diversity 2: most downloaded Minecraft project

> MOST SURVIVAL GAME WINS

Minecraft player gravey4rd had notched up 2,534 wins as of September 2013. That record has since stood for years!

> MOST DOWNLOADED MINECRAFT PROJECT

As of early 2016, this was Diversity 2, created by qmagnet, a special map that challenges you to complete a monument. You can find it here:

www.planetminecraft.com/project/ diversity-2-multi-genre-map

> LARGEST PYRAMID BUILT IN MINECRAFT

Containing 2,629,176 blocks, Stone Titans' pyramid took over a year to build, and is a full reconstruction of the Great Pyramid of Giza. It was declared a world record on 2 November 2013.

> FASTEST TIME TO BUILD A HOUSE

Here's a record you can easily try: the fastest time to build a house using Pocket Edition! The record was set by Tristen Geren of the USA in October 2015. It took him three minutes and two seconds.

> TALLEST STAIRCASE BUILT IN ONE MINUTE

Another Pocket Edition record, Lestat Wade of the USA built a 29-step staircase in 60 seconds in October 2016. The condition of the record is the player must be able to walk up all the steps without having to jump!

Far Lands: longest Minecraft journey

MINECRAFT JOKES

WHAT DID THE CAT SAY WHEN IT WAS GIVEN THREE DINNERS AT ONCE?
Ocelot of food!

WHAT DID STEVE SAY WHEN ALEX ASKED HIM IF HE WANTED TO LEAVE THE OVERWORLD?
I Nether do!

ALEX BROUGHT A LOT OF ROCKS HOME.
She picked them herself!

DID YOU HEAR ABOUT THE MINECRAFT MOVIE?
It's a blockbuster!

RECKON YOU'VE GOT ANY BETTER RIB-TICKLERS THAN THESE?!

STEVE WAS TELLING STORIES OF ALL THE HOSTILE MOBS HE'D BEATEN.
They did drag-on!

ALEX BUILT A HOUSE, BUT IT WAS QUITE SMALL.
Steve said "there's not mooshroom here"!

WHAT'S A CREEPER'S FAVOURITE TIME OF YEAR?
Christmasssssssssssssssssss!

WHAT'S IT LIKE TO HAVE A FIREBALL FIRED AT YOU IN MINECRAFT?
Ghast-ly!

WHAT WOULD STEVE AND ALEX DO WITHOUT TREES?
They wood not know!

57

SSSHHHH! EXPERT MIN SECRETS

Wanna play Minecraft like an expert? Here are six secrets you can use to improve your game in no time!

Get experience!

Farmland can turn back into dirt

You might know that farmland turns back into dirt if it dries out, but it can also be trampled by mobs and players. Avoid jumping on your crops, and you'll keep the farmland blocks ready for planting, saving both time and effort!

Learn the best ways to get experience

Experience in Minecraft is hard to get, because you only get a small amount for everything you do. You can get the most from destroying a monster spawner, but a better option is to dig a large, deep pit beneath the spawner. Mobs will appear then instantly fall, and as long as they're injured but don't die you can easily kill them and get XP.

Build several furnaces

There's no way to speed up the time it takes to smelt a block or cook an item, but that doesn't mean you can't hurry things up. Furnaces are cheap to make (they only need cobblestone and a fuel source), so don't be afraid to build several. Every extra furnace you build halves the total time it takes to smelt the number of blocks you need, so we recommend building at least four for any reasonably sized project.

Mobs can trample farmland

Don't mine when underwater!

ECRAFT

Fishing in the rain means you get bites quicker

Multiple furnaces speed up smelting

Don't mine in water

You can find useful blocks underwater, most notably clay, but mining it isn't advisable since when your top half is submerged, you mine five times slower than when you're on dry land. Even worse, mining blocks underwater can create an undercurrent that stops you swimming fast enough to escape – leave too little time to return for air and you'll drown!

Any expert player knows that there are two things you can do to fix this. You can use enchantments, like Aqua Affinity, to make your time underwater a little easier on you. Or you can place certain items, like doors and fenceposts, which create air pockets underwater that you can stand (and breathe!) in.

Fish when it rains

You can skip rainstorms by sleeping, but experts know that the best time to fish is in the rain. It improves the catch rate of any rod, meaning you're more likely to get your hands on treasure and food. Fishing already takes a long time, so you should only fish during good weather if you're

desperate for food (or fancy relaxing).

You can combine this effect with the Luck of the Sea enchantment for even better results while fishing!

Explore smarter

Getting lost in a cavern is an amateur move for sure. The best way to keep track of where you're going without any extra work is to put torches on only one side of a cavern – left or right is fine, as long as you stick to that. Now, when you want to get back to the surface, just make sure the torches are on the other side of you and you'll be led all the way back without getting stuck.

Put torches on one side of a cave to find your way out

ANSWERS

Dot-To-Dot

Spot The Difference

Blockdoku

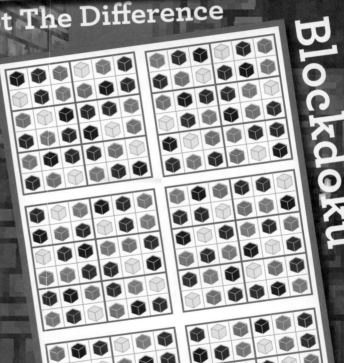

Sword Maze

Craftygrams

1. Polar bear
2. Rabbit
3. Snow golem
4. Silverfish
5. Magma cube
6. Endermite
7. Chicken jockey
8. Wither skeleton
9. Ender dragon
10. Elder guardian

MINECRAFT FACTS

To finish, here are a few Minecraft facts you can use to ~~bore~~ fascinate your friends and family!

MARKUS 'NOTCH' PERSSON
The man who came up with Minecraft!

17 MAY 2009
The day the first ever test version of Minecraft was released for people to play.

18 NOVEMBER 2011
The day the full version of Minecraft was officially released!

$2.5 BILLION
The amount Microsoft paid to buy the company behind Minecraft, Mojang, back in 2014!

DANIEL 'C418' ROSENFELD
The man behind the music of Minecraft.

MINECON
The name of the annual, official Minecraft convention.

OVER 8 MILLION
The number of subscribers Stampy has on his YouTube channel.

2019
The year the official Minecraft movie is set to be released!

OVER 120 MILLION
The number of copies of Minecraft sold worldwide, and growing every day!

365 The number of days we expect to be playing Minecraft in 2018!